ASTRONAUTS

BY DALTON RAINS

Apex is distributed by North Star Editions:
sales@northstareditions.com | 888-417-0195

Produced for Apex by Red Line Editorial.

Photographs ©: NASA, cover, 12, 14–15, 16–17, 18, 19, 20; Robert Markowitz/JSC/NASA, 1, 25; James Blair/NASA, 4–5; Lauren Maples/NASA, 7; James Blair/NASA/SIPA/AP Images, 8–9; CTK/AP Images, 10–11; Bettmann/Getty Images, 13; Megan McArthur/NASA, 21; Jeff Williams/NASA, 22–23; David J. Phillip/AP Images, 24, 29; Melissa Phillip/Houston Chronicle/AP Images, 26–27

Library of Congress Control Number: 2023910439

ISBN
978-1-63738-736-8 (hardcover)
978-1-63738-779-5 (paperback)
978-1-63738-864-8 (ebook pdf)
978-1-63738-822-8 (hosted ebook)

Printed in the United States of America
Mankato, MN
012024

NOTE TO PARENTS AND EDUCATORS

Apex books are designed to build literacy skills in striving readers. Exciting, high-interest content attracts and holds readers' attention. The text is carefully leveled to allow students to achieve success quickly. Additional features, such as bolded glossary words for difficult terms, help build comprehension.

TABLE OF CONTENTS

CHAPTER 1

ASTRONAUT TRAINING

A crane lowers two astronauts into a giant pool. Both wear heavy space suits. They are training for a mission to the Moon.

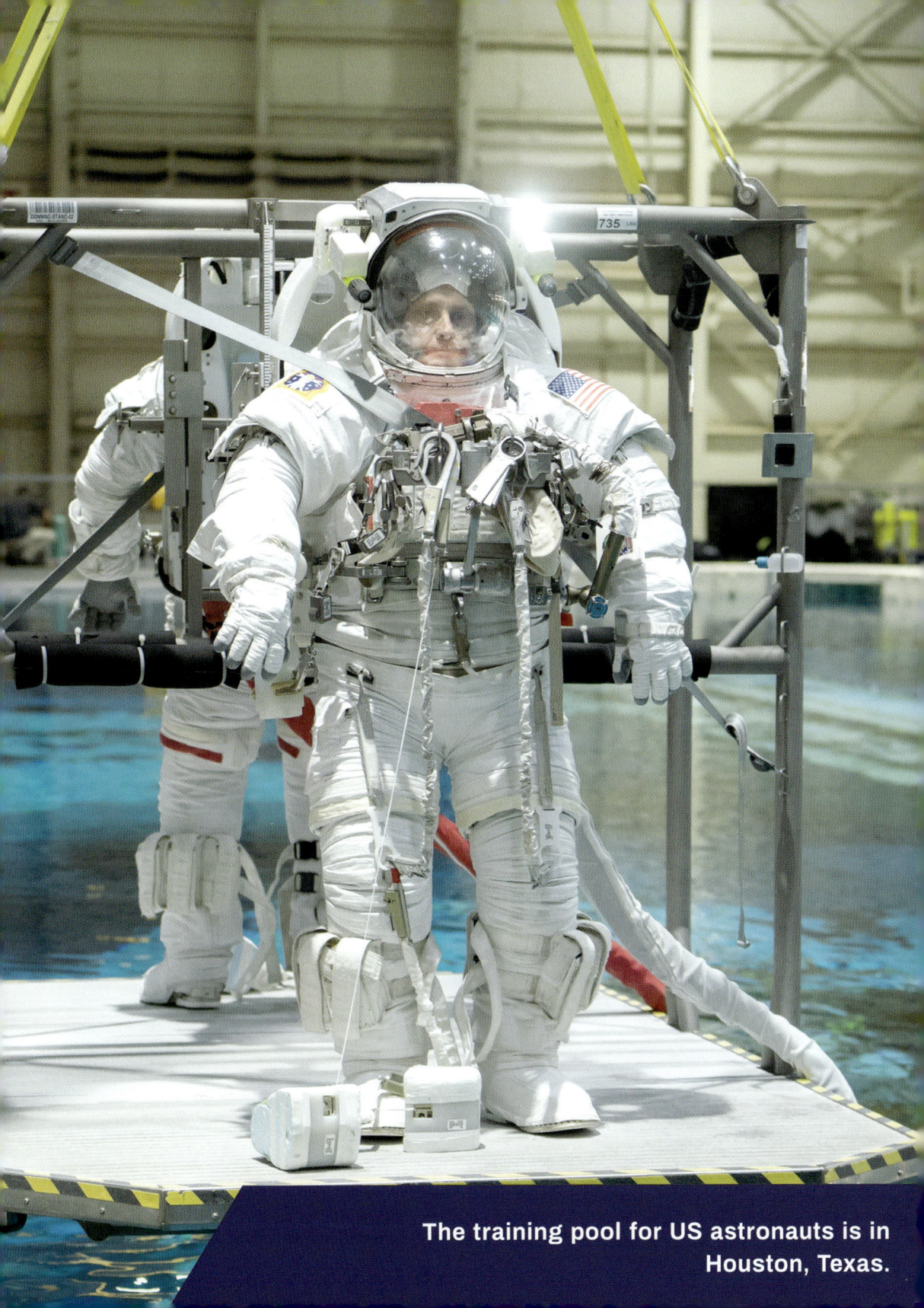

The training pool for US astronauts is in Houston, Texas.

The mission is called Artemis III. It will take the astronauts to the Moon's south pole. Little sunlight reaches that area. So, black curtains keep the training pool dark.

LOTS TO LEARN

Astronauts train for years before missions. They learn how to operate **space stations** and spacecraft. They also study different subjects such as math and geology.

Two people in a dark pool practice being on the Moon's south pole.

Astronauts from all over the world train at the pool in Houston.

The Moon also has lower **gravity** than Earth. Floating in water helps the astronauts prepare. They practice walking and using tools.

FAST FACT

The training pool also helps astronauts prepare for **spacewalks**.

CHAPTER 2

EARLY MISSIONS

Yuri Gagarin was the first person in space. He was from the **Soviet Union**. He orbited Earth in 1961. He circled the planet in about 1.5 hours.

Yuri Gagarin received many honors after going to space.

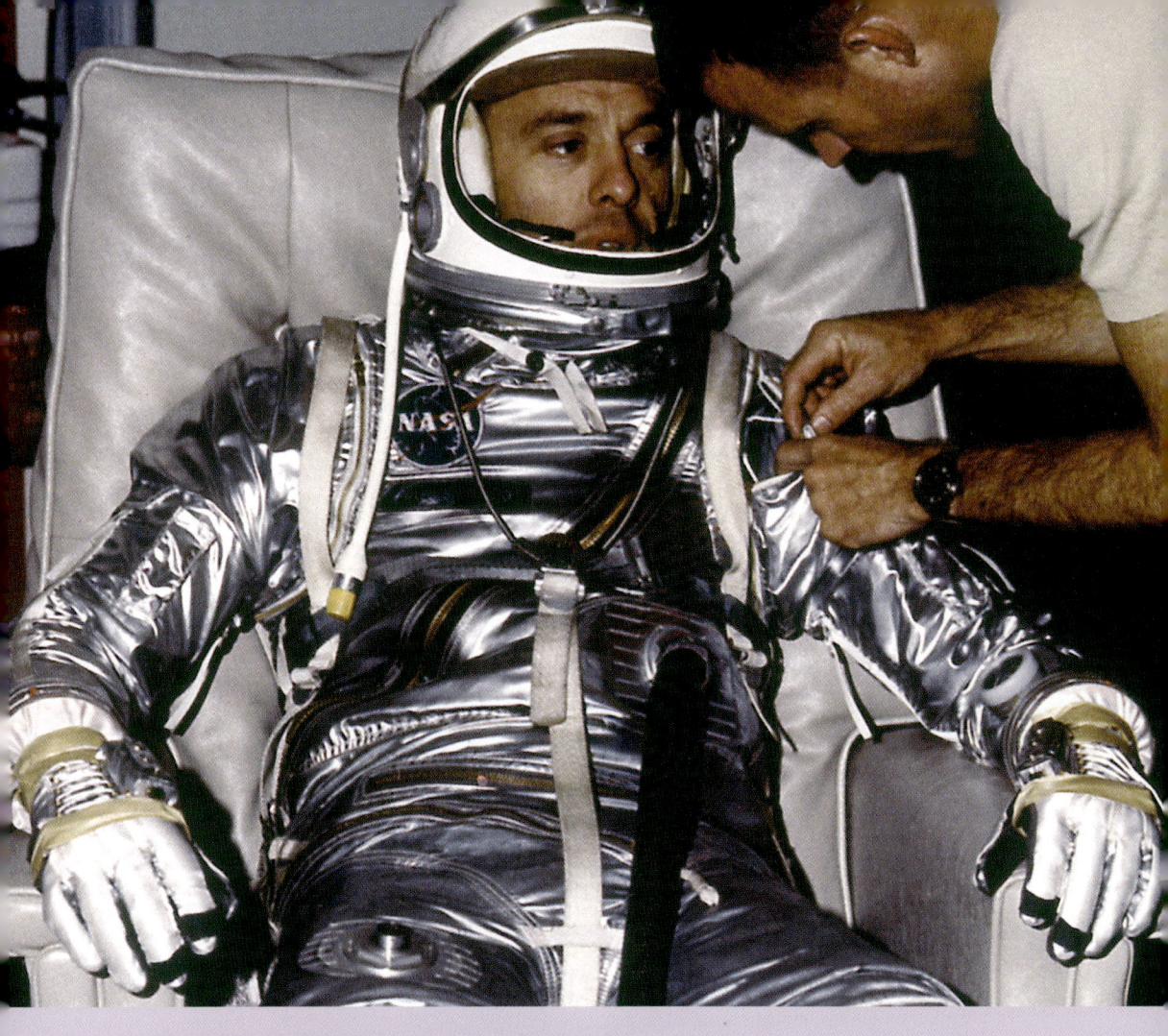

Astronaut Alan Shepard first flew to space on May 5, 1961.

FAST FACT

Alan Shepard's flight lasted less than 16 minutes.

Soon after, Alan Shepard became the first American in space. In 1962, John Glenn circled Earth. He was the first US astronaut to do that.

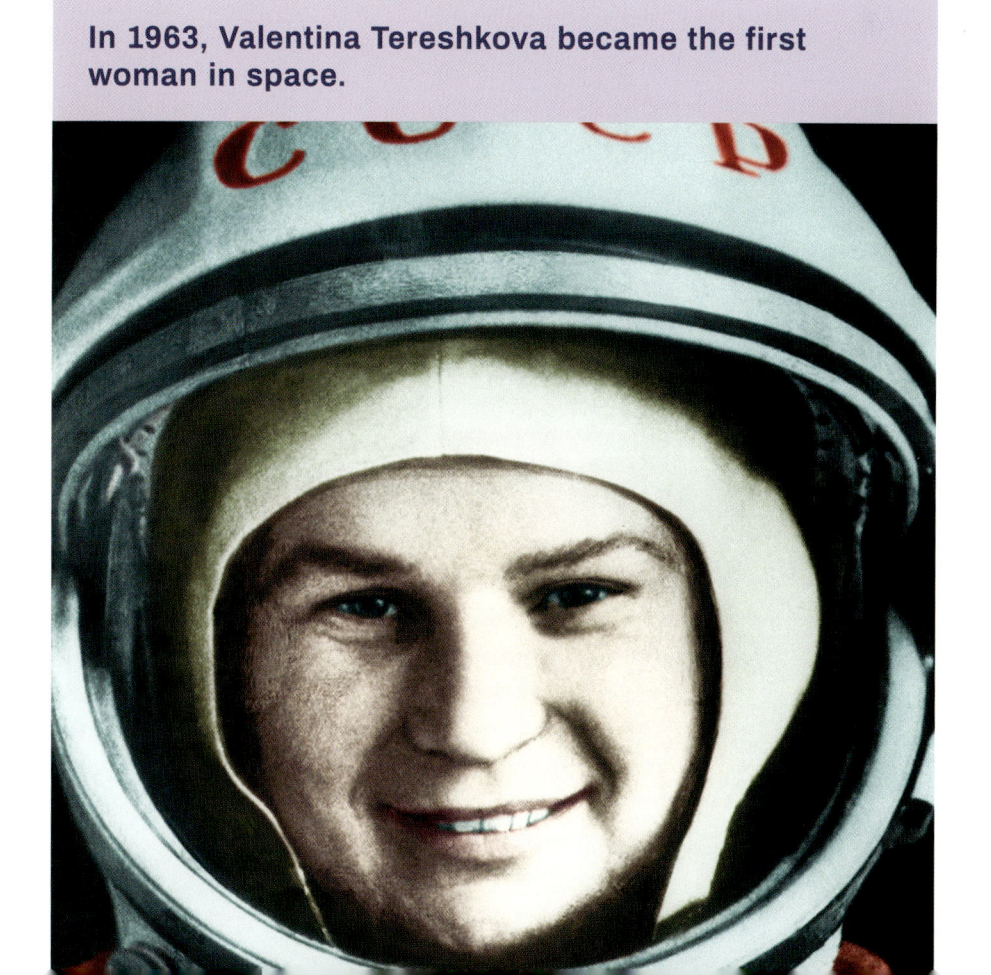

In 1963, Valentina Tereshkova became the first woman in space.

Astronauts wear space suits when they are outside of their ships. That way, they can breathe and stay warm.

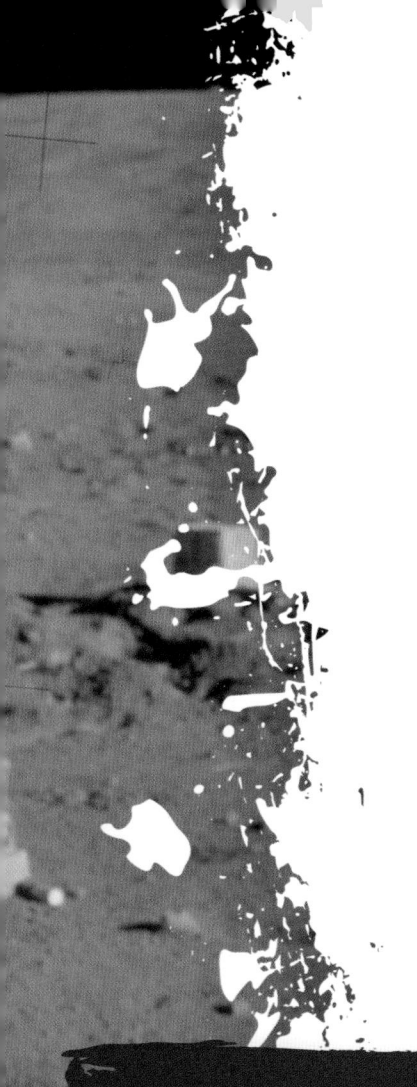

Later, **NASA** began the Apollo program. The program sent several missions to the Moon during the 1960s and 1970s. Twelve astronauts walked on the Moon.

FIRST MOON LANDING

The Apollo 11 mission launched in 1969. Three astronauts circled the Moon. Two of them landed on the surface. Neil Armstrong was the first to walk on the Moon.

CHAPTER 3

STATIONS AND SHUTTLES

In 1971, the Soviet Union launched a space station. Two years later, the United States launched its own. Astronauts could live there. They could stay in space for weeks.

In space stations such as Skylab, astronauts lived and worked in nearly zero gravity.

The space shuttle first launched on April 12, 1981.

The space shuttle began launching in the 1980s. It had a **laboratory**. It also sent astronauts on many missions.

REPAIR MISSIONS

The space shuttle helped with repairs. Some were for the Hubble Space **Telescope**. Astronauts did spacewalks. They fixed some parts. They replaced others.

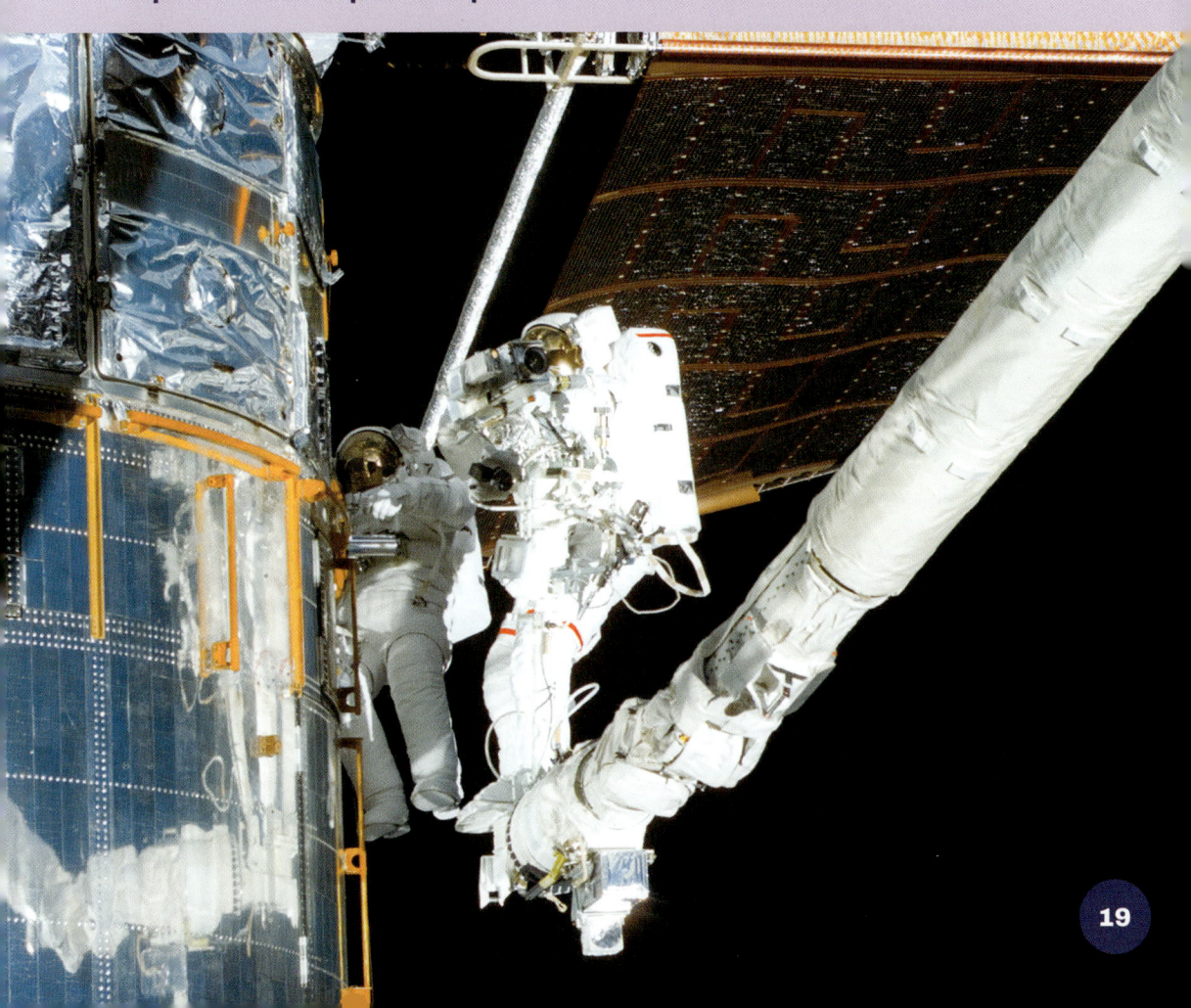

The space shuttle brought astronauts to the Hubble Space Telescope multiple times from 1993 to 2009.

Countries started working together, too. Astronauts built the International Space Station (ISS). They launched one piece at a time. Astronauts assembled the pieces in space.

Construction of the International Space Station began in 1998.

Scientists study many things on the ISS. One is how plants grow in space.

FAST FACT

Astronauts can stay on the ISS for months. They can do long-term experiments.

CHAPTER 4

MORE MISSIONS

n the 2000s, NASA turned more to private companies. It asked them to help send astronauts to space. One company was SpaceX. It built a **capsule**. The capsule brought astronauts to the ISS.

SpaceX's capsule is called the Dragon spacecraft.

NASA hired a company called Axiom Space to make and test new space suits.

Scientists developed new gear for astronauts. For example, they made new space suits. The suits make it easier for astronauts to move around.

FAST FACT

For Artemis III, NASA planned to have the first woman and the first person of color land on the Moon.

NASA announced the Artemis II astronauts in April 2023. This mission came before Artemis III.

NASA helped make a building with an environment like Mars's. People lived alone there for a whole year.

Scientists also wanted to send astronauts to Mars. The trip would take years. So, scientists studied what happens to the human body after a long time in space.

NEW STATION

Scientists made plans for a new space station. It would circle the Moon. They wanted the station to have areas for astronauts to live and work.

COMPREHENSION
QUESTIONS

Write your answers on a separate piece of paper.

1. Write a few sentences describing the main ideas of Chapter 4.

2. Would you like to be an astronaut? Why or why not?

3. In what year did the first astronaut orbit Earth?

    A. 1961

    B. 1963

    C. 1969

4. Why might NASA ask private companies to make parts of spacecraft?

    A. so that NASA can spend more money

    B. so that NASA can focus on other parts of a mission

    C. because NASA is not good at making spacecraft

5. What does **orbited** mean in this book?

*He **orbited** Earth in 1961. He circled the planet in about 1.5 hours.*

    A. lived for a long time in space
    B. took a curved path around an object in space
    C. launched into space from Earth

6. What does **launched** mean in this book?

*The Apollo 11 mission **launched** in 1969. Three astronauts circled the Moon.*

    A. landed
    B. lifted off
    C. crashed

Answer key on page 32.

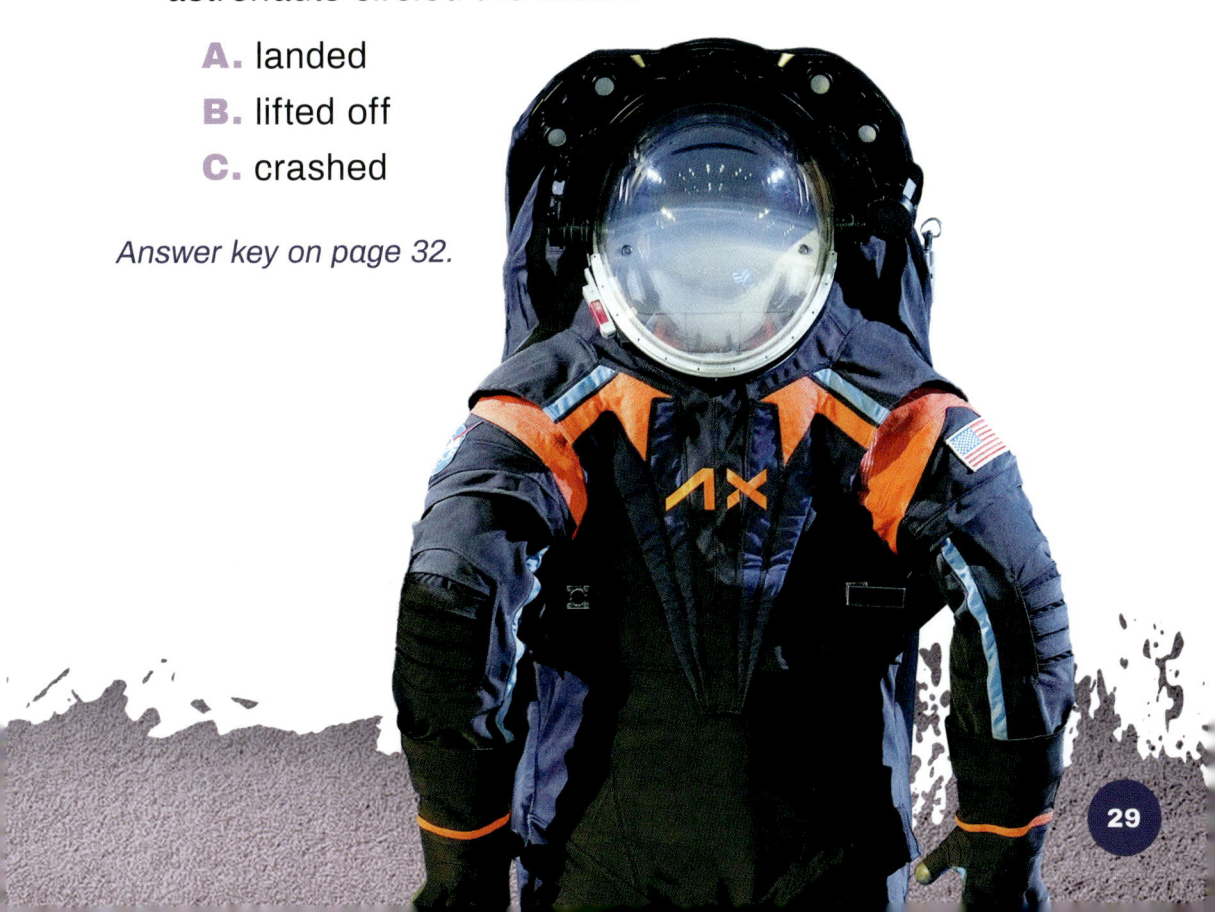

GLOSSARY

capsule
A small spacecraft where astronauts stay.

gravity
A force that pulls objects toward planets, stars, and other objects.

laboratory
A place where people study science, often by running tests.

NASA
Short for National Aeronautics and Space Administration. NASA is the United States' space organization.

Soviet Union
A country in Europe and Asia that existed from 1922 to 1991.

space stations
Spacecraft where astronauts can live. They orbit planets or moons.

spacewalks
Periods of time that astronauts spend outside of spacecraft.

telescope
A tool that helps people see things that are far away.

TO LEARN MORE

BOOKS

Gagne, Tammy. *Space Tourism*. Mendota Heights, MN: Focus Readers, 2023.

Morey, Allan. *Exploring Space*. Minneapolis: Bellwether Media, 2023.

Murray, Julie. *Shuttles*. Minneapolis: Abdo Publishing, 2020.

ONLINE RESOURCES

Visit **www.apexeditions.com** to find links and resources related to this title.

ABOUT THE AUTHOR

Dalton Rains is an author and editor from Saint Paul, Minnesota. He loves to learn about new science discoveries.

INDEX

ANSWER KEY:
1. Answers will vary; 2. Answers will vary; 3. A; 4. B; 5. B; 6. B